AS

Start

TODAY

1-MINUTE DEVOTIONS FOR BUSY BELIEVERS

Al Argo

As You Start Today

1-Minute Devotions For Busy Believers

Al Argo

Ordering Information:
This title can be purchased in bulk for your group or organization.
All proceeds go to create Positive Impact around the world.
For more information contact argoglobal@gmail.com.

––

Publisher's Cataloging-in-Publication data
Argo, Al, 1970-
As You Start Today / Al Argo
p.cm.
ISBN-10: 1974484300
ISBN-13: 978-1974484300

1. Motivational 2. Christian 3. Devotional I. Al Argo II. Title

Printed In The United States of America
10 9 8 7 6 5 4 3 2 1

*Dedicated to busy believers everywhere who
are committed to keeping Christ first.*

*With special thanks and acknowledgement to each of our
prayer and support partners. We are grateful for you!*

"God is in heaven and you are on earth, so let your
words be few."

- Ecclesiastes 5:2

"Father, I pray Your Word will continue to spread, and
Your will be done in each of us."

All verses NIV unless otherwise marked.

Table of Contents

DAY 1

Get Creative

"In the beginning God created the heavens and the earth."

- Genesis 1:1

In the beginning, God created and I happen to believe He is still creating. In fact, the Word teaches that even right now, He is preparing a place for us in Heaven.

If God created the world, the animals, each and every sunrise and sunset, doesn't it make sense that He wants us to walk in His creativity?

It takes creativity to solve problems, make sales, plant a church, raise a family, get out of debt, regain what was lost, etc.

As you start today, ask God to help you walk in supernatural creativity to do the things He calls you to do.

DAY 2

Are You Growing?

"And Jesus grew in wisdom and stature, and in favor
with God and man."

- Luke 2:52

Jesus grew in four distinct areas: wisdom, stature, favor with God
and favor with others.

Is your personal, professional and spiritual growth evident as well?

If not, I encourage you to embark on a path of discovery and discipline
so you can develop as God intends you to grow.

As you grow, you will bear fruit! This is God's desire for you!

However, growth is not easy. It does not happen overnight. It will
not always be fun.

There will be pruning, and there will be growing pains.

This is natural and necessary.

As you start today, ask God to help you grow in
wisdom, stature, and in favor with Him and others!

DAY 3

God Give Me Wisdom

"And Jesus grew in wisdom …"

- Luke 2:52a

Have you ever asked yourself HOW Jesus grew in wisdom?

I imagine He had both a wealth of experiences and classes along with some input from His parents and Rabbi.

We know He studied Hebrew because He read the passage of Isaiah in Hebrew, not Greek or Aramaic.

Have you ever asked yourself HOW you can grow in wisdom?

The Bible encourages us in this way, "If any of you lacks wisdom, you should ask God, who gives generously to all without finding fault, and it will be given to you. " - James 1:5

The ONE thing Solomon asked for was wisdom!

Are you seeking wisdom each day?

We can grow in wisdom by asking God, reading Scripture, reading other devotional books, taking notes in church or the classroom, listening to parents, coaches, mentors, etc.

As you start today, ask God to help you grow in supernatural wisdom beyond your years!

DAY 4

Grow in Stature

"And Jesus grew in wisdom and stature, ..."
- Luke 2:52a

Jesus not only grew in wisdom, He also grew in stature.

Healthy children and teens will grow physically as they consume a proper diet.

Even adults should strive to take care of their body, which the Bible teaches is the temple of the Holy Spirit (I Corinthians 6:19).

Proper and consistent exercise and nutrition will go a long way in helping you grow in "stature."

Jesus was a carpenter.

He certainly was physically active! Are you?

Research shows that a simple thirty-minute to one-hour walk three times a week can dramatically improve your health.

Research also shows that consuming mainly organic fruits and vegetables along with less salt, sugar or protein is one of the best health decisions one can make.

As you start today, ask God to help you grow in stature!

DAY 5

Surrounded in Favor From God

"And Jesus grew in wisdom and stature, and in favor
with God ..."

- Luke 2:52

Jesus GREW in favor! No one can argue with this statement!

It is possible to have more and more and more of the favor of God.

I want more favor from God, how about you?

We are reminded in Psalm 5:12 Surely, Lord, you bless the righteous; you surround them with your favor as with a shield."

Surrounded?

YES! Literally, surrounded with the favor of God!

There is favor, great favor, on your right hand, on your left hand, in front of you and behind you today, tomorrow and forever!

> As you start today, ask God to help you
> continue to grow in God's favor!

DAY 6

Favor From Others

~ ~ ~

"And Jesus grew in wisdom and stature, and in favor with God and man." - Luke 2:52

To grow holistically, we also have to make sure we are growing in our relationships.

It is true, as John Donne wrote, "No man is an island."

We need each other! Sometimes, we may not like each other, but we need each other!

To grow in favor with others, it helps to be diligent, dependable and dedicated.

To grow in favor with others, remember what Steven Covey taught, "Seek first to understand and then to be understood."

To grow in favor with others, also remember what Gary Chapman taught: learn to speak your friends and family members love languages. Is it time, touch, affirmation, gifts or service that makes them feel most loved?

As you start today, ask God to help
you grow in favor from others!

DAY 7

Establish the Work

"May the favorof the Lord our God rest on us; establish the work of our hands for us—yes, establish the work of our hands."

- Psalm 90:17

In the original Greek, the word, "establish", means "to make stable or firm or to confirm."

Establish can also mean "to begin something, to undertake a plan, to give life to an institution, enterprise, etc."

As we start each day, may God establish our work, our projects, our plans and our reputation for His honor and glory.

If our work is stable and firm, we will achieve the results for our company, clients and organization that we desire.

As God confirms our work, He will help us to be fruitful.

As you go about today, keep asking God to let His favor rest on you.

As you start today, ask God to establish
the work of your hands!

DAY 8

Worship the Lord

"Worship the Lord in the splendor of hisholiness"
- Psalm 96:9a

I have been taught that missions exists because worship of God does not yet exist all around the world.

Worship can be expressed as adoration, bowing down to, lifting up of hands to, or being prostrate before the Creator of the universe.

Worship is always you and I loving God.

Worship is always an intimate fellowship with Him.

In fact, the origin of the word "worship" comes from "pros" (for, toward) and "kuneó" (to kiss).

God's desire is that we are close, very close, to Him!

As you start today, ask God to help you worship
Him in the splendor of His holiness.

DAY 9

Press Toward the Mark

"I press on toward the goal to win the prize for which
God has called me heavenward in Christ Jesus."
- Philippians 3:14

I am a huge American college football fan, pulling mostly for my alma mater.

Other members of our church in Asia are rugby or football fans, pulling for various teams in New Zealand, Europe or Asia.

Whatever your team and whatever your sport, I am confident that you want your team to win the championship.

To win, your team must plan, prepare and press on toward the goal.

Your plan for Godly living is found in Scripture!

To prepare,each day, you should put on God's armor and seek God for His will to be done in your life.

Each day, you should press on toward the goal to win the prize for which God has set out for you.

> As you start today, ask God to help you
> press on toward the mark.

DAY 10

Put on the Armor

"Put on the full armor of God, so that you can take your stand against the devil's schemes."

- Ephesians 6:11

To press on, we really do need the armor of God! Do not leave this off!

You need "the belt of truth buckled around your waist" (v 14) and "the breastplate of righteousness in place" (v. 14).

Your feet should be ready with the "gospel of peace," (v. 15) and you also need "the shield of faith, with which you can extinguish all the flaming arrows of the evil one" (v. 16).

Last but not least, each day "take the helmet of salvation and the sword of the Spirit, which is the word of God" (v. 17).

Even with the full armor of God, verse 18 reminds us to PRAY!

As you start today, ask God to truly clothe
you in the full armor of God.

DAY 11

We've Got to Pray

> "And pray in the Spirit on all occasions with all kinds of prayers and requests. With this in mind, be alert and always keep on praying for all the Lord's people."
> - Ephesians 6:18

We need to pray! We need to pray in the Spirit!

We need to pray on ALL occasions!

We need to pray upon rising, driving, working, eating, exercising, before sleeping, etc.

We need to truly follow the Biblical command to "pray without ceasing" (1 Thessalonians 5:17 NKJV).

We need to pray with ALL kinds of prayers and ALL kinds of requests.

There is nothing too big or small to talk to God about it.

Bring it all to Jesus, because He really does care for you.

As you start today, ask God to help you
pray in the Spirit on all occasions.

21

DAY 12

Cast Your Cares on Him

"Cast all your anxiety on Him because he cares for you."

- 1 Peter 5:7

I am not sure what you might be going through right now, but I encourage you to cast all your cares on Him.

The 'what' is not as important as 'Who' you are focused on.

You are not just giving God your anxiety; you are thrusting it, throwing it and casting it to Him.

Do not hold onto your worry! Get rid of it quickly!

Ask God for wisdom, but give your worry, fear and anxiety to Him.

He really does love you. He is concerned for your present and your future.

God cares for you!

As you start today, ask God to help you
cast all your cares upon Him.

DAY 13

Ask For Wisdom

❦ ❦ ❦

"If any of you lacks wisdom, you should ask God,
who gives generously to all without finding fault, and it
will be given to you."

- James 1:5

Wisdom is the principle thing. With wisdom, you will have the right hopes, dreams and goals.

Assume that you lack wisdom! After all, who knows it all?

Ask God for wisdom in various areas of your life!

As you ask, have faith that God is hearing you and giving you the wisdom you seek.

Isn't it great that He gives wisdom "generously to all without finding fault"?

We need wisdom in our attitudes and our actions.

We need wisdom in our relationships and our resources.

We need wisdom in our goals and growth.

We need wisdom in our obstacles and even in our opportunities.

As you start today, ask God to give you
the wisdom that you lack.

DAY 14

Work Heartily

"Whatever you do, work at it with all your heart, as working for the Lord, not for human masters,"

- Colossians 3:23

Do you put your heart into your work?

Do you put your WHOLE heart into your work?

Do not just strive to be the best, strive to do YOUR best.

Don't do it for others; do it for your Heavenly Father.

Work at things, everything, with ALL your heart!

Have a spirit of excellence in everything you do.

If you can do even the smaller things well, the bigger things will work out well!

Seek to improve your knowledge, competency and output.

Can YOU do better? Don't delay, do better for the cause of Christ!

As you start today, ask God to help you to
do everything with ALL of your heart!

DAY 15

Pray Heartily

━━ ❧ ━━ ❧ ━━ ❧ ━━

"Jabez cried out to the God of Israel, 'Oh, that you would bless me and enlarge my territory! Let your hand be with me, and keep me from harm so that I will be free from pain.' And God granted his request."

- 1 Chronicles 4:10

When Jabez prayed this prayer he did not pray an itsy-bitsy-teenie-weenie prayer.

NO! The Bible says he CRIED out to God.

He was not timid. He prayed boldly!

He was desperate for the hand of God to be on his life!

He was desperate for God to show up!

He was desperate for God to intervene!

Are you desperate for the hand of God to be on you, your family and your future?

Are you desperate for God to show up and intervene?

As you start today, ask God to bless you in an
incredible way today and everyday!

DAY 16

Be Strong and Courageous

"Have I not commanded you? Be strong and courageous. Do not be afraid; do not be discouraged, for the Lord your God will be with you wherever you go."
- Joshua 1:9

To be strong and courageous is not just a good suggestion – it is a command!

Don't be afraid! This is a command!

Don't be discouraged! This also is a command!

Be bold! Be encouraged! Take heart! God is with you!

The Lord, YOUR God is with you, and He will continue to go with you!

He will be with you wherever you go.

In the good days and even during what might seem like the worst of times, God is there!

I am reminded of the lyrics to the old song *Be Strong and Courageous* by Michael W. Smith:

> "You know I led your fathers here
> And you know I'll lead you too
> Inscribe my law into your soul
> And nothin' will touch you
> So be strong and courageous..."

As you start today, ask God to help you to
always be strong and courageous!

DAY 17

Got Joy?

"This day is holy to our Lord. Do not grieve, for the joy of the Lord is your strength."

- Nehemiah 8:10b

Today, this day, IS holy to our Lord!

Whatever is going on, remember that the joy of the Lord is your strength.

The JOY of the Lord is your strength.

The joy of the LORD is your strength.

The joy of the Lord is YOUR strength.

Feeling weak? Ask God for His joy!

Feeling down? Ask God for His joy!

You can remember joy as an acronym:

J.O.Y. - Jesus Our Yeshua.

Yeshua is the literal Hebrew word for salvation!

When we accept Jesus as our Savior, there are innumerable benefits!

The JOY of the Lord is just one such benefit.

As you start today, ask God to increase your joy!

DAY 18

Call His Name

"For there is no difference between Jew and Gentile—
the same Lord is Lord of all and richly blesses all who call
on him, for, 'Everyone who calls on the name of the Lord
will be saved.'"

- Romans 10:12-13

First of all, we are all equal.

There is total equality in the eyes of God.

We were all born into sin and therefore totally dependent on Him.

But we hold fast to this promise that He "richly blesses all who call on Him,"

Whatever your income, background, history, skin color, finances, education or looks just call on Him!

He loves you and accepts you as you are. Call on Him!

We hold fast to the promise in verse 13 that "everyone who calls on the name of the Lord will be saved."

He has many names, but all refer to Jesus the Christ:

Adonai, Advocate, Alpha and Omega, Anointed One, The Life, Messiah, etc.

As you start today, call upon the name of the Lord.

DAY 19

This Is the Day!

"This is the day the Lord has made;
We will rejoice and be glad in it."

- Psalm 118:24 (NKJV)

Are you rejoicing or complaining?
Are you moaning and groaning or are you feeling happy and stress-free?
Are you angry or awestruck at the wonder of today?
If you are reading this, you have breath!
You have life! What a wonderful gift we have been given!
You have another day to rejoice and be thankful for!
You and I did not create this day - He did!
We GET to rejoice and be glad in it.
Be glad, not sad. Be glad, not mad.

As you start today, ask God to help you truly
rejoice and be glad all throughout the day!

DAY 20

A Future Hope

"There is surely a future hope for you,
and your hope will not be cut off." - Proverbs 23:18

Ever since I was a teenager, I have had a strong focus on the future.

As an adult, I seek to live each day with all my strength and might, but I am also focused on the future.

Weekly, and often daily, I see various things that are instant reminders for me to pray over my future and my family's future.

Memorize this verse.

Ask God for other reminders to help you remember to pray over your future.

Your future is bright. You are important to God.

Commit your future to Him.

You have a future hope!

Your hope will NOT be cut off!

As you start today, ask God to bless your future in the most remarkable way!

DAY 21

I Can do All Things

∽ ∽ ∽

"I can do all things through Christ who strengthens me."

- Philippians 4:13 (NKJV)

I love the song, *Nothing is Impossible*, by Planetshakers!

"Through You
I can do anything
I can do all things
Cause it's You who give me strength
Nothing is impossible
Through You
Blind eyes are opened
Strongholds are broken
I am living by faith
Nothing is impossible!"

Through Christ you can do anything!
All things ARE possible. Have faith! Believe!
Press on, don't back down and don't give up.
Whatever you need to do today, seek God's supernatural ability to get it done.

Whatever you need to do this year, seek God's supernatural ability to get it done.

Whatever you feel God is calling you to do in your life, seek God's supernatural ability to fulfill His call for your life.

As you start today, ask God to help you
truly do everything through Him!

DAY 22

Best Benefit Package Ever

"Praise the LORD, my soul, and forget not all his benefits—"

- Psalm 103:2

God, the Creator of heaven and earth has also created an amazing benefit package for you and I.

It includes the food on your table, the clothes on your back, the clouds in the sky and even the air that you breathe.

He gave His all, so you and I could experience these benefits and many others!

His grace, mercy, love, and gift of everlasting life are other incredible benefits.

I was once asked by a management group to speak on employee engagement.

This is an important topic, but Christ is the master at engaging His followers and distributing benefits in ways we could never expect.

Let your soul rejoice! Praise the Lord! Do not forget all of His benefits!

> As you start today, ask God to keep revealing
> His amazing benefits to you!

DAY 23

You've Got the Power

"'But you will receive power when the Holy Spirit comes on you; and you will be my witnesses in Jerusalem, and in all Judea and Samaria, and to the ends of the earth.'"

- Acts 1:8

When you are full of the Holy Spirit, you will truly have the power you need to witness and lead others to a right relationship with Him.

Many people crave power, but you can have access to unlimited power as you walk in the presence of the Holy Spirit.

As John Maxwell teaches so well, leadership is influence and I am reminding you that influence is power.

Your power, influence and leadership are simply to help people know about the saving work of Jesus Christ.

Your power, influence and leadership are not only for your hometown, but for the surrounding areas and even other countries.

As you start today, ask God to truly fill you with the power and presence of the Holy Spirit.

DAY 24

Obedience

⤜ ⤜ ⤜

"Now when Daniel learned that the decree had been published, he went home to his upstairs room where the windows opened toward Jerusalem. Three times a day he got down on his knees and prayed, giving thanks to his God, just as he had done before."

- Daniel 6:10

When things go wrong as they sometimes will or when laws are passed that blatantly go against your faith, keep on keeping on!

Do what is right even when it is not convenient.

Do what is right even if it might mean you end up in jail.

Do what is right even if it might mean the lion's den.

Do right! Keep communicating with Him! Keep obeying Him!

Remember the old children's song?

"O-B-E-D-I-E-N-C-E, obedience is the very best way to show that you believe!"

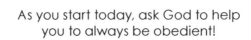

As you start today, ask God to help
you to always be obedient!

DAY 25

Write the Vision

"Then the Lord answered me and said:
'Write the vision And make *it* plain on tablets,
That he may run who reads it.'"
                    - Habakkuk 2:2 (NKJV)

Spend some time in prayer today asking God what He would like you to accomplish in the next 3 to 4 months.

Set a specific date about 3 to 4 months from today. Write the date and a list of things that come to your heart.

Stretch yourself. Dream bigger than you would typically dream.

Ask God to expand your thinking, influence and territory.

Write between 1 to 20 items, or even more if you would like, but do not post the list or share it with anyone.

Make a note to revisit your list in 3-4 months and be amazed at what He has allowed you to accomplish.

As you start today, ask God what He'd like you to accomplish by a specific date 3 to 4 months down the road and write these things down.

DAY 26

You Become Like Who You Hang Around

"Blessed is the one who does not walk in step with the wicked or stand in the way that sinners take or sit in the company of mockers"

- Psalm 1:1

Want to be blessed? Watch the company you keep.

Do not walk 'in step with the wicked' – do not follow in their footsteps.

Do not 'stand in the way that sinners take' – do not be like them.

Do not 'sit in the company of mockers' – this is not good either, is it?

You are encouraged to be a witness to unbelievers, but your closest friends should be people who are also close to Him.

Did you know your attitudes, actions and even your finances closely resemble the attitudes, actions and finances of your five closest friends?

> As you start today, ask God to give you Godly friends with whom you can serve the Lord.

DAY 27

Want to Be Blessed?

"But whose delight is in the law of the Lord,
and who meditates on his law day and night."

- Psalm 1:2

Want to be blessed? Delight yourself in the law of the Lord.

Meditate on His Holy Word both day and night.

You can post Scripture in your bathroom, car dashboard, locker, office, mirror, etc.

You can memorize Scripture and read Scripture throughout the day.

Reading, posting and memorizing Scripture is a great way to delight in and meditate on the Word of God.

What do you do to meditate on the Word at night?

Before I was married, and now if I am traveling alone, I often listen to an audio Bible as I sleep.

You will be blessed as you delight in and meditate on the Word of God.

As you start today, ask God to help you
delight in and meditate on His Word.

Day 28

Prosper

"That person is like a tree planted by streams of water, which yields its fruit in season and whose leaf does not wither—whatever they do prospers."

- Psalm 1:3

When you and I are careful who we associate with (knowing we become like who we hang around) and when we delight in and meditate on the Word of God; the Bible says we will become like a "tree planted by streams of water."

We will bear fruit in season!

Our leaves will not wither!

Whatever we do will prosper!

What a powerful word picture!

What a wonderful promise!

It does NOT say 'most' of what we do will prosper, it says 'whatever' we do will prosper!

As you start today, ask God to help everything you do to prosper.

DAY 29

The B-I-B-L-E!

"All Scripture is God-breathed and is useful for teach-
ing, rebuking, correcting and training in righteousness"
- 2 Timothy 3:16

Every word you read in the Bible is inspired by God Himself.
It is God-breathed!
If you want knowledge and wisdom, read the Bible!
If you need a "kick in the pants", read the Bible!
If you know you have missed the mark and need a little (or a lot) of
course correction, read the Bible!
The best training manual there ever was, is in fact, the Bible!
Remember this old children's song?
"The B-I-B-L-E, yes, that's the book for me,
I stand alone on the Word of God, The B-I-B-L-E!"

As you start today, ask God to speak to you
as you read and study His Word.

DAY 30

Your Future Is Bright!

"'For I know the plans I have for you,' declares the Lord, 'plans to prosper you and not to harm you, plans to give you hope and a future.'" - Jeremiah 29:11

God has some amazing plans for you!

He has plans that we cannot even dream or imagine at this point!

He has plans to prosper you!

He has NO plans to harm you!

He has amazing plans to give you a hope and a fantastic future!

He has declared this and He is God! He cannot lie!

Your future is important! Your future is bright in a right relationship with Him.

Not our will, but His will be done in our future!

Keep praying, praying, praying over your life and your future!

As you start today, ask God again to bless your future!

DAY 31

The Best Laid Plans

"In their hearts humans plan their course,
but the Lord establishes their steps."

- Proverbs 16:9

There is nothing wrong with planning!

In fact, we will soon see that we should plan, prepare and proceed to follow the plan we feel God is leading us too.

As we follow Christ, we can rest assured that He is establishing our steps.

Sometimes we might have a flat tire, be delayed in traffic or miss a flight.

We do not want any of these things to be our fault, but if it happens, we should remember that "all things work together for good to those who love God" (Romans 8:28).

There is a purpose for everything that happens.

You might get to meet someone you would never have met and that person may even accept Christ.

You might miss an accident you would have been in if not for the delay.

As you start today, ask God to bless your plans
and establish your steps today and forever!

DAY 32

Stretch Your Imagination

"Now to him who is able to do immeasurably more than all we ask or imagine, according to his power that is at work within us"

- Ephesians 3:20

God can do more when we come to Him with our inability, shortcomings, failures and our lack than if we proceed with pride and arrogance in our own ability.

Life is not about us, but about His power working within us.

When we allow Him to work through us we will see great things accomplished in His name.

He can do greater things then we could ever ask, dream or imagine!

Stretch your Godly imagination!

Ask God, "What is impossible that You would like me to try?"

Write down what you hear Him speaking!

As you start today, ask God to do more through you than you could have ever imagined.

DAY 33

He Gets the Glory

> "To him be glory in the church and in Christ Jesus
> throughout all generations, for ever and ever! Amen."
>
> - Ephesians 3:21

Whatever happens, God gets the glory!

No matter what happens in your local church or the worldwide body of Chris, He get the glory.

He gets the glory in all Christ has done and is doing.

He gets the glory through all past, current and future generations.

He gets the glory forever and ever!

All glory belongs to Him.

Remember, it is "His power that is at work within us," (Ephesians 3:20)

This is reason enough for you and I to give Him praise, honor and glory, right?

As you start today, ask God to really help
you give Him the glory He deserves.

DAY 34

Two Are Better Than One

"Two are better than one,
Because they have a good reward for their labor:"

- Ecclesiastes 4:9 (NKJV)

You can do more with a partner than by yourself.

Your spouse, your business partner, your friends and family are all vital relationships that you should nurture.

The author of Ecclesiastes continues his thought in verse 10 saying,

"For if they fall,
one will lift up his companion.
But woe to him who is alone when he falls,
For he has no one to lift him up."

It truly is better to have someone with whom you can talk to, partner with, strategize with and do life with.

Do you have someone?

As you start today, ask God to bless those in your life and, as He desires, to bring others into your life as well.

DAY 35

A Good Name

"A good name is better than fine perfume"

- Ecclesiastes 7:1a

Fine perfume can make you smell nice, but a good name follows you when your character is right.

Companies spend billions protecting their brand name.

Celebrities spend millions on publicity to promote or enhance their name recognition.

The book of Proverbs is correct when the author wrote in Proverbs 22:1,

"A good name is more desirable than great riches;"

Better then the best perfume and better then great riches is a good name.

Names always convey meaning!

What meaning do you truly wish for your name to convey?

As you start today, ask God to help you have a good name.

DAY 36

Holy Moly!

"Do not be overrighteous, neither be over wise – why destroy yourself?"

- Ecclesiastes 7:16

Don't be overrighteous.

Don't be self-righteous.

To do so might lead you to being prideful which comes before a fall.

God has called us to holiness, but true holiness must start with our inner heart before expressing itself through our attitudes and actions.

Some people still teach that women wearing dresses is an act of holiness.

Others still teach that drums are, in and of themselves, unholy.

Some teach that to be holy, you cannot even use electricity! Wow! Can you imagine?

As you start today, ask God to help you to be real
and to be really holy but not overrighteous.

DAY 37

Sharpen Your Saw

"If the ax is dull and its edge unsharpened, more strength is needed, but skill will bring success."
- Ecclesiastes 10:10

You can do a job with the proper tools, but if you have wisdom you will also take care of the tools that take care of you.

Now, more than ever before, we are living in a knowledge-based economy. Your most important tool is your mind.

We need to sharpen our mind, intellect and Spirit so we can accomplish all that He wants us to accomplish.

Strength is important, but skill means you can conserve some strength and be even more productive.

As you start your day, ask God to help you
sharpen your saw for His glory today.

DAY 38

God Is Ambidextrous

"So do not fear, for I am with you;
do not be dismayed, for I am your God.
I will strengthen you and help you;
I will uphold you with my righteous right hand."
- Isaiah 41:10

Do not fear! He is near! Do not be discouraged or dismayed! He is your God!

He promises to strengthen you! He promises to help you!

If you feel weak, ask Him for His strength!

If you need help today, ask Him! I am always asking!

He has promised to uphold you with His righteous right hand!

If He is upholding us with His right hand, what do you think He is doing with His left?

Fighting our battles? Protecting us? Leading and guiding us? All this and more!

As you start today, ask God to strengthen you
and help you as you go throughout the day.

DAY 39

One Thing

"One thing I ask from the Lord,
    this only do I seek:
that I may dwell in the house of the Lord
    all the days of my life,
to gaze on the beauty of the Lord
    and to seek him in his temple."

- Psalm 27:4

There is just one thing! It is the main thing! There is nothing else.
We have to seek this! We have to ASK for this!
Anything and everything else is just peripheral.
Nothing else really matters!
Our strongest desire should be to commune with Him,
To dwell in His house all the days of our life,
To look upon His beauty, His holiness, His majesty,
And to be with Him in His temple.

As you start today, ask God to help you stay
in His presence all the days of your life!

DAY 40

Commit to the Lord

❧ ❧ ❧

"Commit your actions to the LORD, and your plans will succeed."

- Proverbs 16:3 NLT

What are you planning on doing today?

Commit it to the Lord!

Whether you are working, attending class, going scuba diving or sky-diving, commit it to the Lord so He will establish your plans.

Just give it to Him.

Ask Him to bless your day!

Go ahead, talk to Him.

He may respond with a gentle nudge, a soft whisper or direct you to a verse in the Bible.

He may respond by giving you great weather or by allowing you to have a flat tire on your way to your event.

Who knows what your day may hold? He does!

Commit to the Lord whatever you are intending to do today, and allow Him to establish your plans!

As you start today, ask God to establish your plans!

DAY 41

A Verse for Our Neighborhood

"Dear friend, I pray that you may enjoy good health and that all may go well with you, even as your soul is getting along well."

- 3 John 1:2

Our family and our neighborhood need this prayer!

As I write this we have just returned from the ER with our 14-year old son Chandler.

Another 14-year old, Merlin, down the road has been sick a week and another neighbor, Barb has also been battling sickness for too long!

We have other friends from the USA, Japan, Thailand and the Philippines who are also persevering through struggle.

I pray that each person reading this, and each person you know from your friends to your family members may enjoy good health!

I pray that all may go well with you!

I pray that your soul will prosper today, tomorrow and forever!

As you start today, ask God to give you good health, that all may go well with you and that your soul may always prosper!

DAY 42

Petitions, Prayers, Intercession and Thanksgiving

❧ ❧ ❧

"I urge, then, first of all, that petitions, prayers, intercession and thanksgiving be made for all people"

- 1 Timothy 2:1

First words and last words are important!

Paul, as he wrote this letter to Timothy, was very precise in his first words.

"I urge" implies a plea or a sense of urgency! What he says next is deemed important!

"First of all" simply means that other things are coming but what he is saying first is of utmost importance!

"That petitions, prayers, intercession and thanksgiving be made " bluntly states to do all! Not just one or the other.

We are to offer petitions (requests) to God for others.

We are to pray for others!

We are to intercede (stand in the gap) for others!

We are to offer thanksgiving to God for others!

"For all people" means for all people! Those we like. Those we don't like. Those we know. Those we might not know. Those who are literally naked and those who are wearing Prada.

As you start today, ask God to help you pray, intercede and give God thanksgiving for all people!

DAY 43

A Great Friend

"A friend loves at all times,
and a brother is born for a time of adversity."

- Proverbs 17:17

Everybody needs a good friend!

My family is so blessed! My wife and I both have close friends we have known since high school.

My children have close friends they have known for many years.

We have been blessed with amazing neighbors!

We literally have friends scattered across the globe in the most amazing places.

A friend loves at all times, even when the going is tough.

A brother or a sister is great to have in a time of difficulty or adversity.

As you start today, ask God to help you be a great friend and to give you amazing friends for life!

Day 44

He Is for You

"What, then, shall we say in response to these things?
If God is for us, who can be against us?"

- Romans 8:31

God is for you! He is on your side!

He knows you and is pulling for you.

He is fighting for you and with you.

Indeed, He has your back, and He is watching over your future.

What else can we say? If He is for us, who can be against us?

There is at least one against us, and he goes about like a roaring lion seeking whom he can devour (1 Peter 5:8).

But he is powerless in the presence of Jehovah.

What about you? Are you always for Him? Are you on His side?

Are you fighting the good fight?

As you start today, thank God that He is always for you, and ask Him to allow you to always be for Him.

DAY 45

New Every Morning

> "Because of the Lord's great love we are not con-
> sumed, for his compassions never fail. They are new every
> morning; great is your faithfulness."
>
> - Lamentations 3:22-23

God has an incredible great love for us!

Because of this love, we have made it through yet another night!

He is good! We are not consumed! We have life and life more abundantly!

Promises! Amazing promises!

We claim these promises for us, our friends, and our entire family!

We even have promise of eternal life as we place our trust in Him!

His compassion toward us will NEVER fail!

His compassion toward us is new every morning!

Thank you Father for your great faithfulness!

As you start today, ask God to again show you His compassion and thank Him for His faithfulness.

DAY 46

My Shepherd

"The Lord is my shepherd, I lack nothing.
He makes me lie down in green pastures, he leads me beside quiet waters"

- Psalms 23:1-2

The Lord is your shepherd! He is leading you and guiding you in the way you should go!

He really likes you, and He loves you so much!

Praise Him now because He is protecting, feeding, and nurturing you!

As your Shepherd, He provides for all your needs according to His riches in glory (Philippians 4:19).

You lack nothing.

As a child of the Most High, you are able to lie down in beautiful, lush green pastures.

You are able to rest in peace along the quiet, still waters!

As you start today, ask God to continue to meet all your needs, and allow you to rest when it is time to rest!

DAY 47

Refresh

"He refreshes my soul. He guides me along the right paths for his name's sake. Even though I walk through the darkest valley, I will fear no evil, for you are with me; your rod and your staff, they comfort me."

- Psalm 23:3-4

As you start today, understand that only
Christ can truly refresh your soul!

His desire for us is so strong that today He is willing and able to guide you along the right path.

He is doing all this because as Christians, we bear His name!

Yes, sometimes we may go through dark places and challenging times, but we should never fear evil.

It cannot touch us! Our Shepherd is always with us!

His rod and staff is there to lead, protect and comfort us as we go along today's journey.

As you start today, ask God to refresh your soul
and to lead you along His right path!

DAY 48

Your Goodness and Love

"You prepare a table before me
in the presence of my enemies.
You anoint my head with oil;
my cup overflows.
Surely your goodness and love will follow me
all the days of my life,
and I will dwell in the house of the Lord
forever."

- Psalm 23:5-6

Even in the midst of anguish and adversity, Christ is there!

Even as terrorism and violence increases, as a child of God, you are able to feast at the table of the Lord.

Christ is anointing your head with oil today.

His touch is all you need.

With His portion, your cup will continually overflow!

His goodness and His love will follow YOU, all the days of your life!

His desire is for you to dwell in His house forever and ever!

As you start today, ask God to anoint you and to
overtake you with His goodness and love!

DAY 49

Be Strong and Courageous

> "'Be strong and very courageous. Be careful to obey all the law my servant Moses gave you; do not turn from it to the right or to the left, that you may be successful wherever you go.'"
>
> - Joshua 1:7

Want to be successful? I mean really successful?
Be strong! Be courageous! Be careful to obey all the commands of God!
Stay on the straight and narrow! Do not turn from His way one iota.
You are on an amazing quest!
Do not bear to the left or veer to the right!
Focus on your faith and loving God and loving people!
Do this and you will not just be successful, but you will be excel in whatever you do and wherever you go!

As you start today, ask God to help you to be strong, courageous and to help you obey all that He has instructed you to do.

DAY 50

Always on Your Lips

"Keep this Book of the Law always on your lips; meditate on it day and night, so that you may be careful to do everything written in it. Then you will be prosperous and successful."

- Joshua 1:8

Want to be prosperous? Again, do you want to be successful?

This is not man talking - this is the Word of God!

We either have to accept it or deny it.

The Bible teaches that to be prosperous and successful, you have to keep the Bible hidden in your heart and 'always on your lips.'

This is your key to being blessed beyond stress.

Meditate on God's word both morning and evening, so you will know the treasure it contains and how you should obey and apply it to your daily life.

As you start today, ask God to help you meditate on and memorize the Word of God today, tomorrow and forever!

DAY 51

Water

"But whoever drinks the water I give him will never thirst. Indeed, the water I give them will become in him a spring of water welling up to eternal life." - John 4:14

As you wake up this morning, one of the most important things you can do is drink a nice, clean, cool cup or two of refreshing water.

Ahhhh, water!

How much more important to drink from His cup!

Water refreshes! His Word refreshes!

Water nourishes! His Word nourishes!

Water brings amazing health benefits! His Word brings amazing health benefits!

Water boosts your mood! His Word boosts your mood!

Water helps eliminate fatigue! His Word helps eliminate fatigue!

Water flushes out toxins! His Word flushes out toxins!

Water brings life! His Word brings eternal life!

As you start today, ask God to give you more of His incredible life-giving water!

DAY 52

Food

"'My food,' said Jesus, 'is to do the will of him who
sent me and to finish his work.'"

- John 4:34

Physical food is important, but what really filled Christ up was to do
the will of Him who sent Him AND to finish His work!

Like all of us, Jesus ate because He was hungry. He ate for nourishment. He ate for energy.

What fills you up? What gives you nourishment? What gives you
energy?

Christ's focus was not only on 'doing' the work, but on 'finishing' the
work.

If we focus on finishing, then we will finish each day well.

Christ started well, and He also finished well.

Remember, as children of God, whatever we do is part of God's work.

As you start today, ask God to help you do His will and
finish His work, no matter what you need to do today.

DAY 53

A Gentle Answer

"A gentle answer turns away wrath, but a harsh word stirs up anger."

- Proverbs 15:1

He is still working on each of us.

It is one thing to know you should do something, but it is a completely different thing to actually do what you know.

As leaders, fathers, wives or teachers, we know that a gentle answer turns away wrath; however, most of us do not always respond with a soft answer but sometimes we give a harsh, hard or angry response.

Aren't you glad God answers you with a gentle answer?

Aren't you glad, He is good enough to be gentle with you and tough with His enemies?

Your family, students or employees are not your enemies.

Give a soft, gentle answer more often than not, and if you are going to be angry, be angry but "do not sin" (Ephesian 4:26).

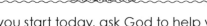

As you start today, ask God to help you
respond in a soft and gentle manner.

DAY 54

No Weapon

"'No weapon forged against you will prevail,
and you will refute every tongue that accuses you.
This is the heritage of the servants of the Lord,
and this is their vindication from me,'
declares the Lord."

- Isaiah 54:17

You will always face obstacles, but these obstacles will not prosper.
Any weapon formed against you will not prevail!
Any false accusation will be proved false!
Any evil word spoken against you will not come to pass.
You are a beloved child of God.
He loves you and has spoken words of life and life more abundantly for your future.
As a believer, you are washed in the blood of the Lamb.
Old things have passed away.
No devil in hell or on earth can prevail!

As you start today, ask God to destroy any weapon
that has been formed against you and to reverse
any curse that has been spoken over you.

DAY 55

His Thoughts! His Ways!

"'For my thoughts are not your thoughts,
neither are your ways my ways,' declares the Lord."
- Isaiah 55:8

Wouldn't you agree with me today that His thoughts are better than our thoughts?

His ways are better than our ways.

We are so limited, yet we can do all things through Christ.

We are so powerless, yet we have power after the Holy Spirit has come on us.

We are born with a sinful nature, yet we are washed in His blood.

He is still thinking amazing thoughts for us and our future.

He has amazing plans for your future.

Do not loose heart!

Don't give up; that is not the way you should go.

Press on! Pray on! Keep on keeping on!

As you start today, ask God to show you a glimpse
of His good and loving thoughts toward you.

DAY 56

Don't Loose Heart

"Therefore we do not lose heart. Though outwardly we are wasting away, yet inwardly we are being renewed day by day."

- 2 Corinthians 4:16

I once met a man in Singapore who had lost his wife, job and entire financial stability.

He literally thought he had lost it all and was on the verge of losing his heart.

I met him in his taxi and was able to encourage him to not lose heart. This is my encouragement for all of us today – do not lose heart!

H.E.A.R.T. is an acronym to:

Hear the Word. (Read and listen to God's Word.)

Enter into the Word. (Put yourself in the story of the Bible.)

Act on the Word. (Just obey.)

Relay the Word. (Share the Word with others.)

Trust the Word. (Keep trusting and obeying.)

As you start today, ask God to renew you today and to never let you lose heart.

DAY 57

In All Your Ways

"Trust in the Lord with all your heart,
and lean not on your own understanding;
In all your ways acknowledge Him,
And He shall direct your paths."

- Proverbs 3:5-6 (NKJV)

Are you trusting in Him with all your heart?

Sometimes our greatest challenge is to trust and obey, yet, there is still no better way!

Remember, His thoughts are higher then your thoughts, so do not lean on your own understanding!

Today, in everything we do, we need to submit our will and our way to Him.

"In all your ways" means at work, school, relationships, athletics, goals, etc.., in EVERYTHING!

When we do this, He has promised to make our paths straight!

As you start today, ask God to help you trust in
Him and submit to Him in all your ways.

DAY 58

Peace

"Peace I leave with you; my peace I give you. I do not give to you as the world gives. Do not let your hearts be troubled and do not be afraid."

- John 14:27

What do you currently have in your possession? What do you own?
One thing that you can have for certain is PEACE!
Christ gave it to you! He left it with you as a gift.
Whatever happens, do not let your heart be troubled!
Do not be afraid! Hold onto His hand and cling to His peace.
It truly does pass all understanding!
Money without peace is true poverty.
A marriage without peace is only turmoil.
A day without peace is absolute misery.
A life without peace is anything but peaceful.
A life without Christ leads to crises.
I remember this saying from when I was a teen:
"No Christ; No Peace! Know Christ; Know Peace!"

As you start today, ask God to fill your heart
and mind with His amazing peace.

DAY 59

Today

"As long as it is day, we must do the works of him who
sent me. Night is coming, when no one can work."

- John 9:4

What is the most important thing you need to do for Him today?

What is the most important thing you want to do for Him during your lifetime?

Maybe His desire for you is to speak healing over a blind person.

Maybe His desire for you is to be instrumental in providing clothes for the naked.

Maybe His desire for you is to lead a businessman into a relationship with Him.

Whatever you have on your agenda today, work at it with all your heart.

Let all your work be done as for the Lord.

As you start today, ask God to help you
work wholeheartedly for Him today!

Day 60

The Greatest Commandment

"'Love the Lord your God with all your heart and with all your soul and with all your mind and with all your strength."

- Mark 12:30

As disciples who follow Christ, we are commanded to love the Lord with our whole being.

Our heart, soul, mind and strength must be completely sold out to Him.

We must love Him with all our being.

Gary Chapman, in The Five Love Languages, teaches that as humans we receive love through time, touch, affirmation, gifts and service.

For you and I, it is possible to spend time with Christ.

It is possible to let Him reach out and touch you.

We can praise Him and speak words of affirmation to Him.

We can bring gifts to Him as an act of worship.

We can serve Him all the days of our life.

As you start today, ask God to help you love Him
with all your heart, soul, mind and strength!

DAY 61

Hear Me

"Hear me, Lord, and answer me, for I am poor and needy."

- Psalms 86:1

Today, let this be your heart's cry.
God hear me! God listen to me.
I am poor when compared to your great wealth, influence and worth.
I am needy in so many different ways.
I need You! I need You more today than ever before.
On behalf of my family, future and oh, so much more, I need you God.
Answer me when I call upon you today.
Hear me! Listen to my every word.
Thank you, Father for hearing my heart and answering me!

As you start today, ask God to hear you
and answer your every prayer.

DAY 62

Guard Me

"Guard my life, for I am faithful to you; save your servant who trusts in you. You are my God"

- Psalms 86:2

Father, my prayer today is that you will truly guard my life.

Lord, You know I am not perfect, but by your grace, I am faithful.

I am full of faith though sometimes it might only be the size of a tiny mustard seed.

I trust in You with all of my heart, mind and soul.

You are my God! You are my Father! You are faithful!

You know no limitations; You know no boundaries.

You can guard my life, and I am asking you to continue doing so today and forever!

As you start today, ask God to guard your
life today, tomorrow and forever!

75

DAY 63

All Day Long

"Have mercy on me, Lord, for I call to you all day long."

- Psalms 86:3

Mercy is defined in the dictionary as "compassion or forgiveness shown toward someone whom it is within one's power to punish or harm."

Thank God for His compassion and forgiveness!

While there are several Greek and Hebrew words for the Biblical word "mercy", the most common usage originates from the Hebrew word "hesed", which represents God's covenant of loving kindness.

God has mercy on His children.

He is full of love, compassion and kindness toward you.

His mercies are new every morning and all day long.

As you start today, ask God to show you His mercy and keep calling on Him all day long.

DAY 64

Just Dance

"Bring joy to your servant, Lord, for I put my trust in you."

- Psalms 86:4

The joy of the Lord is our strength!

We need joy, happiness and gladness so we can truly rejoice in Him.

Remember, only He can really bring us true joy!

The only person to trust in today is Christ alone!

Whatever happens from the sunshine to the rain, trust in Him.

Whatever happens from happiness to pain, trust in Him.

He can turn your mourning into dancing (Psalms 30:11) and your dancing into destiny.

Sometimes you just gotta dance!

You may not feel like it, want to or think you need to, but just dance!

As you start today, ask God to bring you joy
and receive all the He has for you.

DAY 65

Amazing Love

"You, Lord, are forgiving and good, abounding in love
to all who call to you."

- Psalms 86:5

Yes, you are forgiving! Yes, Lord you are so good!

Your abounding, overflowing, and never-ceasing love is absolutely amazing!

We call on You now with all our heart, soul and mind.

Hear us and answer us today, oh God!

Many are our sins and shortcomings. Forgive us Lord!

You know that we are far from perfect, but mold us and make us into Your perfect image!

Great is Your love for all of us! Shower it down more and more!

As you start today, ask God to shower
you with His amazing love today!

DAY 66

Surprise Blessing

"May God be gracious to us and bless us
and make his face shine on us –
so that Your ways may be known on earth,
Your salvation among all nations."

- Psalm 67:1-2

This is my prayer for today and everyday: God be gracious to me and bless me indeed!

Surprise me, and surprise all who are reading this, with your amazing blessings today!

Make your face shine upon us, so we can reflect your love and glory!

Lord, bless us so Your ways might be known throughout all the earth!

Lord, let your salvation be known among all the nations, tongues, tribes and people groups.

We are blessed to be a blessing. Bless us today Lord!

As you start today, ask God to be
gracious to you and to bless you!

DAY 67

Come to Jesus

"'Come to me, all you who are weary and burdened, and I will give you rest. Take my yoke upon you and learn from me, for I am gentle and humble in heart, and you will find rest for your souls.'"

- Matthew 11:28-29

Are you tired or burdened today?
Does the weight of the world seem to be on your shoulders?
Run to Christ and He will give you rest.
Walk to Christ and He will comfort you.
If you can't run or walk, get there ever how you can.
Call on Him and He will answer you!
You will find rest for your body, mind and soul in Him!
He is gentle and humble in spirit.
There is much we can learn from Him today, and it begins when we come to Jesus!

As you start today, ask God to help you draw near to Him!

DAY 68

Strength, Power and Stamina

"He gives strength to the weary
and increases the power of the weak.
Even youths grow tired and weary,
and young men stumble and fall;
but those who hope in the Lord
will renew their strength.
They will soar on wings like eagles;
they will run and not grow weary,
they will walk and not be faint."

- Isaiah 40:29-31

When you are tired, keep going!
When you fail, keep growing!
When you are fired - keep working!
When you are lost, keep searching!
Put your hope in Him to renew your strength!
It is time for you to soar on wings like eagles.
It is time for you to run, and walk, and not be weary!

> As you start today, ask God to give you
> strength, power and stamina!

DAY 69

In All Your Ways

"Trust in the Lord with all your heart
    and lean not on your own understanding;
in all your ways submit to him,
    and he will make your paths straight.
Do not be wise in your own eyes;
    fear the Lord and shun evil."

- Proverbs 3:5-7

There are things we may think we understand, but do not rely on your understanding!

There are things beyond man's understanding, but God knows and understands!

Today, put your hope and full trust in Him.

Trust in Him with all your heart, mind and soul.

In everything you do and everywhere you go, acknowledge Him, submit to Him, and He will direct your paths!

Do not consider yourself wise in your own eyes. This simply means you are not as wise as you may perceive.

Seek wisdom; ask Him for wisdom and guidance!

As you start today, ask God to help you
trust Him and submit to Him!

DAY 70

Good God

"You are good, and what you do is good;
teach me your decrees."

- Psalm 119:68

In good times and in bad, He is still God and He is still good!

In health and sickness, poverty and riches, He is still good and He is still God!

Whether we acknowledge Him or not, He is still God!

We serve a good, good God!

He is good and what He does is good.

God, teach us your law, your commands and your decrees!

As you teach us, let us be quick to obey because we know that obedience is better then sacrifice!

As you start today, praise Him for His goodness!

As you start today, ask God to teach you His decrees!

DAY 71

May the Nations Be Glad

"May the peoples praise you, God;
    may all the peoples praise you.
May the nations be glad and sing for joy,
    for you rule the peoples with equity
    and guide the nations of the earth."

- Psalms 67:3-4

My prayer for today is that all the people of the earth will praise the Lord!

My prayer is that there will be peace, happiness and joy in every nation.

My prayer is that every tongue, tribe and ethnic group will sing for joy to Him.

He is the One who promoted true equity before the foundation of the world!

He has promised to guide each nation of the earth.

When we welcome Him by our side, He will be our faithful guide!

As you start today, ask God to bless your nation, surrounding nations and all the nations and leaders on the earth.

DAY 72

Seeds

"May the peoples praise you, God;
  may all the peoples praise you.
The land yields its harvest;
  God, our God, blesses us.
May God bless us still,
  so that all the ends of the earth will fear him."

- Psalm 67:5-7

Praise and worship belongs to Him alone!

In times of planting, nurturing and harvesting, He deserves our praise!

The land will yield its harvest!

The Lord will bless you!

The Lord will bring the increase.

He will multiply!

He can do exceedingly, abundantly much more with our seeds then we can do with an entire harvest.

What can you do with a single seed? Eat it on a salad?

But if you plant it, He will allow it to multiply.

There is a time to plant, a time to harvest and a time to eat.

The earth will see the blessing of the Lord and be drawn to His holy name!

As you start today, ask God to bless the
seeds you have been planting!

DAY 73

Content, Confident and Courageous

❧ ❧ ❧

"Keep your lives free from the love of money and be content with what you have, because God has said,
    'Never will I leave you;
    never will I forsake you.'
    So we say with confidence,
    'The Lord is my helper; I will not be afraid.
    What can mere mortals do to me?'"

- Hebrews 13:5-6

Are you content? There is nothing wrong with money but there is everything wrong with the love of money and discontentment.

He has promised to never leave us nor forsake us!

We can confidently declare that He is our helper!

Have no fear, for He is near.

Others might threaten or try to intimidate us, but they cannot harm you or I.

Be content! Be confident! Be courageous!

Be content with what you have and what you have accomplished if you have done your best.

Be confident in who you are and in Whose you are!

Be courageous today, tomorrow and forever as you continue to serve Him through serving others!

As you start today, ask God to make you content, confident and courageous!

DAY 74

Strength and Defense

"'The Lord is my strength and my defense;
  He has become my salvation.
He is my God, and I will praise him,
  my father's God, and I will exalt him.'"

- Exodus 15:2

Your Father, your God is your strength, your song and your mighty defense!

He is your salvation! He is worthy of your praise today!

He is a good, good Father: faithful, attentive, trustworthy, holy, everlasting and righteous!

He knows how to give good, good gifts to you, His child!

He loves to spend time with you.

He loves it when you long for His gentle touch.

His attention is on you, and He longs for your attention as well.

He is serving you today, tomorrow and forever.

As you start today, ask God to be your strength, song and defense! Ask God to be your Father!

DAY 75

His Faithfulness

❧ ❧ ❧

"Know therefore that the Lord your God is God; he is the faithful God, keeping his covenant of love to a thousand generations of those who love him and keep his commandments."

- Deuteronomy 7:9

As you start today, know that He is faithful!

He is faithful to keep all his promises and His covenant of love to a thousand generations of those who love Him and obey Him.

His promises are yes and amen! Every one is true!

You can count on every word!

Do you know this?

Do you really believe it with all your heart, mind and soul?

He is faithful to you, your future and all creation!

Psalms 36:5 says that His love reaches to the heavens and His faithfulness to the skies!

As you start today, ask God to help you
be more aware of His faithfulness!

DAY 76

Hello

"'Call to me and I will answer you and tell you great
and unsearchable things you do not know.'"

- Jeremiah 33:3

Our God, being the loving, caring parent that He is, is always attentive to you!

When we call out to Him, we have a powerful promise that He will answer us and even show us great and unsearchable things that we are not even aware of.

Just as good parents are always aware of their children's wants, needs and desires, God too is aware of our wants, needs and desires.

Call on the name of the Lord, and He will hear you!

As you start today, ask God to help you be attentive
to those around you as He is attentive to you.

DAY 77

Trust Him

"In you our ancestors put their trust;
they trusted and you delivered them.
To you they cried out and were saved;
in you they trusted and were not put to shame."

- Psalm 22:4-5

Whether you are a first generation child of God or come from a long line of Christ followers, know that your spiritual forefathers trusted in Him.

As we place our hope and trust in a trustworthy Father, we will never be disappointed.

The key is to trust in Him with all of our hearts and lean not on our own understanding (Proverbs 3:5).

When we trust wholeheartedly, we will never ever be put to shame.

As you start today, ask God to help you trust
Him with all your heart, mind and soul!

DAY 78

Holiness

"But just as he who called you is holy, so be holy in
all you do; for it is written: 'Be holy, because I am holy.'"
- 1 Peter 1:15-16

We serve a holy God whose desire for us is that we might be holy and whole as well.

When we are wholly His, we can be His holy children.

We are indeed called to walk in holiness.

This is not perfection, but it is purity.

It is not about never making a mistake, but it is being in the world but not conformed to the world.

So many people allow the world to influence them, while they live in the world.

Holiness is being in the world, but not of the world!

As you start today, ask God to make
you holy just as He is holy!

DAY 79

Be Kind

"Be kind and compassionate to one another, forgiving each other, just as in Christ God forgave you."

- Ephesians 4:32

Today, be kind! Be kind, gentle and compassionate!

Today, be quick to forgive! Be nice!

Everyone makes mistakes. Everyone has shortcomings.

Mother Teresa once said, "If you treat everyone like they are hurting, you will be right 99% of the time."

Everyone stumbles and falls.

It is impossible to hold a grudge without allowing the grudge to also hold you back.

Release your inner kindness today.

Be nice to the stranger, but especially those who share your house and workspace.

Pay kindness forward, even before others do a kind deed for you.

As you start today, ask God to help you
be kind and compassionate.

DAY 80

Words and Meditation

"May these words of my mouth and this meditation of my heart be pleasing in your sight, LORD, my Rock and my Redeemer."

- Psalm 19:14

What words will you use today?

Words can heal or words can wound.

Words can build a person up or tear a person down.

Words are powerful.

What are you thinking about?

What are you meditating on?

I have heard it said over and over, "you become what you think about most of the time."

What do you think about most of the time?

Think about that question.

Let's meditate on Him so we become more like Him!

As you start today, ask God to bless the words of your mouth and the meditation of your heart.

DAY 81

Teamwork

"Whatever happens, conduct yourselves in a manner worthy of the gospel of Christ. Then, whether I come and see you or only hear about you in my absence, I will know that you stand firm in the one Spirit, striving together as one for the faith of the gospel."

- Philippians 1:27

Do you act each day in a manner worthy of the gospel of Christ?

This means not only walking in personal obedience but also walking in corporate unity.

Working, walking and fellowshipping together so that you can "stand firm in the one Spirit."

Christian teamwork is implied and commanded.

Who are you working with?

Who are you fellowshipping with?

Who are you intentionally avoiding?

The verse is clear that we are to strive "together as one for the faith of the gospel."

As you start today, ask God to help you work, walk and fellowship with fellow believers for a greater witness, relationship and impact.

DAY 82

Our Shield

"'Every word of God is flawless;
he is a shield to those who take refuge in him.'"

- Proverbs 30:5

Every promise of God is absolutely true!

Every word of His is flawless! It is completely without error.

He is a shield to all who take cover in Him!

He is our refuge and our rock!

He is our salvation, stronghold, and Savior!

He will protect, cover and keep us safe as we trust and obey Him.

Sometimes we might be tempted to disobey, but do not fall to the temptation.

Trust and obey!

Even in the smallest things, trust and obey.

Small decisions made correct today add up to a significant life tomorrow.

As you start today, ask God to be your shield
as you journey throughout the day.

DAY 83

Lifetime Favor

"For his anger lasts only a moment,
  but his favor lasts a lifetime;
  weeping may stay for the night,
  but rejoicing comes in the morning."

- Psalm 30:5

What makes God angry? Not the sinner, but the sin.

What makes God happy? Not just the good deeds, but the doer of the good deeds!

You are His child!

TODAY and for the rest of your life, receive His favor!

There are some days when you may need to cry.

Go ahead and cry. Give it all to your Father!

But know that there will soon come a time when you can truly rejoice as well!

It is morning; rejoice in Him today.

As you start today, ask God to give you a lifetime
of favor and to make today a day of rejoicing!

DAY 84

Our Ever Helper

"God is our refuge and strength,
an ever-present help in trouble."

- Psalms 46:1

Have you ever heard it said that good help is hard to find?

God is our refuge! He wants us to run to Him and take cover in His dwelling place.

He IS our strength.

When we are weak, He strengthens us!

When you need help, ask Him!

He is always here to help.

From schoolwork to housework, He can help you along the way!

From the office to the playing field, He is your refuge, strength and help!

From wisdom to finances, He is listening and guiding you each day!

As you start today, ask God to help
you every step of the way!

DAY 85

Crazy Things

> "And we know that in all things God works for the good of those who love him, whohave been called according to his purpose. For those God foreknew he also predestined to be conformed to the image of his Son, that he might be the firstborn among many brothers and sisters."
> - Romans 8:28-29

Sometimes crazy things might seem to happen.

Thirteen days before marriage, my fiancé's house burnt down with all of our wedding gifts and joint worldly possession inside.

About 17 years later, my wife and I experienced a major earthquake and one of the world's worst typhoons within a two-week span.

Now that we have been married for over twenty years, there are many more stories.

Yet, the message remains the same: God is working things out for our good and the good of those around us.

You and I are both called according to His purposes!

Before the foundation of the world, He knew us!

As you start today, ask God to truly work all things out for your good as you go throughout the day.

DAY 86

Impossible?

"Jesus looked at them and said, 'With man this is impossible, but with God all things are possible.'"
- Matthew 19:26

What might seem impossible to you, in your own power, is possible with God.

God is not limited by time, space, place, finances, knowledge or anything else for that matter.

God can work out all these things, even through you.

He always works it out for His honor and glory.

What situation are you facing that seems impossible?

Ask God to work it out for His glory!

Right now, my North Carolina mom is facing a situation that the doctors may call impossible.

But, we declare her healed in Jesus name.

Right now, a Christian coffee house we are building in Asia seems impossible.

But we call it complete and open in Jesus name.

What impossible situation are you facing?

Ask Him to work it out for His glory!

As you start today, ask God to make the impossible possible!

DAY 87

Guard Your Heart

"Above all else, guard your heart, for everything you
do flows from it."

- Proverbs 4:23

There is nothing more important than for you to guard your heart.

Do not entertain things that ought not be entertained.

If you do not guard your heart, who will?

If you are a teen, your parents cannot guard your heart.

If you are an adult, your spouse cannot guard your heart.

Only you, with the help of God, can guard your most important possession - your heart.

Everything else you do, think, say or imagine flows from your inner heart.

Guard your heart with everything within you so that your inner being and your health, finances and future will prosper.

As you start today, ask God to help you to guard your heart!

DAY 88

Freedom

"It is for freedom that Christ has set us free. Stand firm, then, and do not let yourselves be burdened again by a yoke of slavery."

- Galatians 5:1

Are you free?

If so, walk in your freedom!

We were once all bound by sin and separated from God.

But the Bible teaches that as we come to Him, as we put our faith and trust in Him, He will set us free.

We also know that he who the Son sets free is free indeed.

Do not go back on the old path; keep on keeping on!

The old path is full of burdens, barriers and breakups.

The new path is full of freedom, forgiveness and fellowship.

Walk in your freedom, experiencing and expressing the true joy of the Lord.

As you start today, ask God to always help you walk in His freedom!

Day 89

Seek Good

"Seek good, not evil,
    that you may live.
Then the Lord God Almighty will be with you,
    just as you say he is."

                                            - Amos 5:14

Do you want to live a long, happy and prosperous life?
Seek good and not evil!
Seek God, and seek good.
Seek God for yourself, and seek good for others.
Seek good for your future, your family and your faith.
Run from evil; don't pursue it!
Evil is just the devil without the "d".
Evil is vile! It is just plain wicked!
Love God; hate sin!
Let Jesus reign; never let evil in.
As you pursue good and pursue God, He will always be with you, and that is what you really want, isn't it?

As you start today, ask God to help you
to seek good today and forever!

DAY 90

The Greatest Commandments

> "'Love the Lord your God with all your heart and with all your soul and with all your mind and with all your strength.' The second is this: 'Love your neighbor as yourself.' There is no commandment greater than these."
> - Mark 12:30-31

We are not perfect, but as we love the Lord with all our heart, soul and mind, we are going to get better.

As we love our neighbor as ourselves, we (and they) will also get better.

Above all else, love God!

After that, before anything else, love people.

Love God and love people!

Have you heard that before?

Easy to say, yet hard to implement.

Implement it daily through your attitudes and actions.

Speak life into each of your relationships.

Encourage those you meet.

Grow in love!

Grow in love toward God and others.

As you start today, ask God to help you love Him with everything you have and to love others as much as you love yourself.

DAY 91

Fly Like an Eagle

～ ～ ～

"But those who hope in the LORD
will renew their strength.
They will soar on wings like eagles;
they will run and not grow weary,
they will walk and not be faint."

- Isaiah 40:31

Eagles are majestic creatures!
When you hope in your Creator you also will renew your strength.
You will soar above your problems like an eagle soars above the earth.

Eagles are known for their:
1) Vision - Eagles can spot friend or foe up to 50 miles away. How is your vision?

Remember where there is no vision, the people perish.

2) Vitality - Eagles live a vibrant life but around age 30 they do grow tired and weak.

They retreat to a safe place and shed their feathers and beak and and emerge 5 months later full of life again. Are you keeping a weekly Sabbath where you can renew and energize your life?

3) Vigilance - Eagles are vigilant and watchful. Have you ever heard the term 'eagle-eye'?

Watch and be aware of what is entering your mind and heart.

4) Viciousness - Eagles mate for life and are great parents, but they are vicious when it comes to their enemies.

Do not let the wiles of the enemy get the best of you. Let the boldness of the Lord rise up in you to destroy the work of your flesh.

5) Victories - Eagles live a victorious life, which is also what God has called you to walk in!

As you start today, ask God to help you hope in Him and to renew your strength so you can soar on wings like eagles!

DAY 92

Consider the Ant

⚉ ⚉ ⚉

"Go to the ant, you sluggard;
consider its ways and be wise!
It has no commander,
no overseer or ruler,
yet it stores its provisions in summer
and gathers its food at harvest."

- Proverbs 6:6-8

Have you really ever considered the way of the ant?
Here are 4 quick facts about ants that we can apply to our lives:

1) Ants are powerful - Ants can lift the equivalent of 50 times their body weight.

If we could do that, we could toss full sized cars with the ease we can currently throw a soccer ball. God makes you powerful when you put your faith, hope and trust in Him. You really can do all things through Christ.

2) Ants are persistent - Block the path of an ant and they will go around, over or under the obstacle.

We all have obstacles. The challenge is to discover the opportunity within each obstacle.

3) Ants are protectors - A typical job for an ant is to be a nurse, forger, cleaner or soldier.

All four jobs have to do with the relative long-term survival of the ant colony. You also have a great task of being a nurse, forger, cleaner and soldier for your spouse and family. How are you doing protecting the ones you love?

4) Ants are planners - Ant colonies can be relative in size to NYC or Atlanta.

In fact, ant colonies can stretch for literally thousands of miles. Ants think winter in the summer and their engineering skill is so legendary that much of the current robotics field is derived from the study of ants. Are you planning your short and long-term goals?

Be a planner!

As you start today, ask God to help you consider
the ways of the ant so you can learn to be wise.

SUPPORT THE ARGO'S MINISTRY TODAY!

≈ ≈ ≈

Since 2001, the Argo family has served full time with World Missions Ministries. During this time they have traveled to such places as Cuba, Canada and China and to other various parts of Asia including Nepal, Malaysia and Philippines. As the A-Team, their mission is to Teach, Equip, Activate and Mobilize the Asian church to finish the Great Commission. (John 4:34) Their focus is on church planting, coffee house ministry, leadership training and publishing. They rely on consistent prayer and generous monthly support to continue, and expand, the work God has called them to. Please partner with them as the Lord leads through your prayer and giving.

Checks (marked with Argo #28061-S) or support for Life Coffee House & Library (marked #24019-P) can be mailed to:

World Missions Ministries,
PO Box 270420,
Oklahoma City, OK 73137

For secure online giving please visit: www.bit.do/give2misisons or give. iphc.org/argo-al

All gifts are tax-deductible.

All gifts, including legacy and memorial gifts, are acknowledged and appreciated.

Personal letters or correspondence can be sent to:

Al Argo
PO Box 123
Falcon, NC 28342

Al can also be reached by email at argofamily@yahoo.com

YOUR written review on Amazon.com, Audible.com, iTunes or Goodreads can help others discover this & other titles by Al Argo
   Look for *Wake Up & Shine, 160 Super Sales Success Tips or Walking, Living, Learning* available now.
   Look for *The Word, Wisdom & Worship - 365 Days of Devotions* available in 2018.

Made in the USA
Las Vegas, NV
19 July 2021